Reaching Out
To Immigrant
Parents

Cristina Casanova

Cover Design — Linda Jean Thille

Editor — Dianne Schilling

Copyright © 2002, Revised 2010,
Innerchoice Publishing • All rights reserved

ISBN – 10: 1-56499-069-3

ISBN – 13: 978-1-56499-069-3

INNERCHOICE PUBLISHING
15079 Oak Chase Court
Wellington, FL 33414
(877) 799-5350
Email: info@innerchoicepublishing.com

Reaching Out To Immigrant Parents

What others are saying:

"I highly recommend this important and timely book. As our schools and country become more and more culturally diverse, this book will help counselors and educators to support children's healthy development and capacity to learn."

Jonathan Cohen, Ph.D
President, The Center for Social and Emotional Education
Teachers College, Columbia University

"Ms. Casanova — who is remarkable to meet in person — does an equally notable job of defining many of the family and cultural issues that must be considered by educators of immigrant children. As a valuable primer on immigrant cultural considerations, including trauma histories, *Reaching Out to Immigrant Parents* is must-learning for anyone seeking involvement and cooperation from our newest citizens."

Jim Schmidt
Vice President and CEO, Sidran Institute for Traumatic Stress Education and Advocacy

"Wow! This little book packs a punch. As the author reminds us, 'An ounce of research is worth a pound of contrition.' Casanova's research, insight, and years of experience pay off. The reader can learn what's important in under an hour; the impact of trauma exposure and culture shock on immigrant students and their parents, and what to do to help these students to be successful. Engaging stories and practical advice make this book readable and useful."

Ricky Greenwald, Psy.D.
Director of Training, Children After-Trauma Care and Health Program
Mount Sinai School of Medicine

"Once I started reading this timely book, I couldn't put it down. It is extremely well written from a practical, knowledge-based and personal point of view. The comprehensive, yet succinct, approach to understanding the complexity of the immigrant experience and the sensitivity needed to work with parents is a much needed addition to the counseling field.

"I applaud Cristina for synthesizing critical concepts and research in a clear and concise manner. The case-study approach in which the culture quiz is presented allows the reader to deepen his or her understanding of how to effectively communicate with immigrant parents.

"This is a significant book that must be read by all those who truly wish to better understand how to work with immigrant parents who are new to this country."

Priscilla Chavez-Reilly
Supervisor of Guidance, New York City Board of Education

"Welcoming families as vital partners in the school community can create a stimulating learning environment. It can also be frustrating and challenging, especially when social customs and mores, language differences, even fear become barriers that can hinder this partnership.

"Cristina Casanova offers eye-opening insights into the many challenges that are unique to immigrant families in her ground breaking book, *Reaching Out to Immigrant Parents*. Her hands-on approach provides educators and counselors with communication guidelines, comprehensive cultural factors, parent outreach ideas, tips for conducting a parent meeting, suggestions for parent-child activities, and an exciting gamut of ideas that motivate the reader to become culturally skilled and knock down the barriers."

Cathrine Kellison McLaughlin
Author, The Do's and Don'ts of Parent Involvement'

Dedication

To my grandmother, Maria Arguel, with whom I share the forced immigration experience as well as its gifts and sorrows.

Contents

Chapter 1

Introduction

Many years ago, when I was a counselor working as a parent-child mediator, I learned a poignant lesson about cultural sensitivity that I have never forgotten.

Typically, when a student is having ongoing conflicts with a parent, or when the child is experiencing difficulties in school that require parental monitoring or assistance, the counselor schedules a parent-child conference. Wearing her mediator cap, the counselor seats the child on one side of the table and the parent on the other side. She then takes a position between the two and facilitates communication until the problem is clarified and a resolution defined.

In this particular situation, I was concerned about a Vietnamese student who was not doing well in school, so I phoned and scheduled a meeting with his father. When the father arrived, I showed him to the meeting room and followed the usual protocol, with all three of us sitting at the same table.

I noticed as the meeting progressed that the father was not making eye contact with either his son or me. Most of the time he was staring down at his folded hands on the table. And, although the father agreed to every decision that was made, he contributed very little to the discussion.

At the close of the meeting, I scheduled follow-up appointments with the father. He understood that he was expected to return, but never did.

Puzzled, and certain that I had done something wrong, I contacted a social service agency that works with Asian immigrants. The social worker I spoke with had no trouble pinpointing two significant mistakes I had made with this father — one a violation of the power relationship between the father and son, and the other relating to my female gender.

From the viewpoint of this Vietnamese father, whose beliefs and values still largely reflected his native culture, being asked to sit at the same table with his son, and carry on a discussion as though the two of them were equals, was unthinkable (and a breach of culturally acceptable "power distance," a concept that will be discussed later in this book). The perceived loss of authority was humiliating to the father.

My second mistake, which greatly compounded the first, was to assume that a female could mediate between two males. In the Vietnamese culture, men enjoy significantly greater status than women. Although I would not have defined my mediator role as a power position (helper or facilitator is more like it), this father perceived me as having overriding authority in the situation. For a woman to put him in such a demeaning position in front of his son was mortifying.

How should this situation have been handled? Had I not attempted to conduct a joint meeting, with father and son at the same table, it is entirely possible that the father would have accepted me in my role as counselor. After all, he had some knowledge of how U.S. educational institutions are structured. So simply meeting separately with the father and son was one alternative (though I'd forfeited that option with my initial blunder). An even better approach would have been to ask a male counselor to meet with the father, while I worked with the son. This, in fact, was the solution I chose—albeit after the fact.

However, first I had to apologize. I contacted the father, admitted my mistakes, pleaded ignorance, and asked him to give the system another try. Then I arranged to have a male colleague meet with the father, while I counseled the son. While this approach required more time and energy than the typical three-way mediation, it did produce positive results, one of which was that I never made the same mistake again.

When working with immigrant parents, I don't take anything for granted. An ounce of research is worth a pound of contrition.

My experience with the Vietnamese father is not unique. Cultural conflicts like this happen hundreds of times a day in schools throughout the United States. Sometimes they are satisfactorily resolved, but many times they go completely unnoticed, and every time that happens an opportunity to improve the educational experience of a student is lost.

In the 1970's our country experienced a sudden surge in the influx of Southeast Asian families. But it was just that — a surge in the steady flow of immigration that has been going on since before the birth of our nation. The U.S. was a country of immigrants at its founding, and the cultural kaleidoscope keeps turning and changing — always challenging our institutions to adjust and accommodate.

Schools are among the first institutions to absorb the cultural fluctuations brought about by immigration.

The number of first generation immigrants living in the United States has gone from

9.6 million in 1970, to over 38 million in 2007. According to New York City Board of Education statistics, the New York schools enroll students from more than 140 countries who speak over 170 different languages and/or dialects. In visiting classrooms you would see students from Asian, Slavic, Arabic and Spanish-speaking countries. Each of these groups in turn represents a multitude of unique backgrounds and experiences.

Immigrant students are entering an unfamiliar realm where the dominant values and practices may be alien to their prior life experiences. This can result in significant feelings of confusion and isolation. For better or worse, acculturation begins immediately, but the process can be frightening and chaotic unless the student senses the support and understanding of a welcoming staff and student body.

Struggles may arise as students attempt to merge their culture's views with the predominant American perspective, especially in the following areas:

- Gender equity
- Authority roles
- Cultural practices (attire, food, religious practices, holidays, etc.)
- Respect for parental authority
- Family expectations and cohesiveness

- Relative openness in expression of feelings, beliefs and ideas
- Conflict management style
- Individualism versus group identification
- Language barriers

In many cases, immigrant students prove surprisingly resilient and eager to mimic the behaviors and values of their American peers. Some come from countries where Western culture has already made significant inroads, whether through television, movies, music, technology or MacDonald's. However, too rapid acculturation can often spell trouble at home, as conflicts develop between children intent on change and parents determined to preserve traditional values.

This book is about reaching out to immigrant parents because it is often the parents, not the students, who need the greatest understanding and help. School systems differ around the world. In many countries parent involvement is not expected, or wanted. Immigrant parents may not understand how the U.S. school system works and be totally unfamiliar with the concept of parent involvement. In addition to not understanding the school system they often have very little knowledge of how to support their children's educational development.

Few children, regardless of culture, achieve their full academic, social and leadership potential without the support of a caring, involved family. Talented, able immigrant children can easily fall by the wayside if their parents are so alienated from the educational system that they are unable to assist with homework, language acquisition, and a whole array of compliance issues ranging from simple attendance to behavior codes and discipline policies. When parents are in overt (or covert) conflict with the educational system, the cultural tug-of-war for the mind and heart of the child can be devastating.

By extending a welcoming hand, making efforts to communicate, and involving immigrant parents in the schooling of their children, we can circumvent many of these problems. It's a preventive approach, really, one that attempts to support and strengthen the child at the foundational level.

As educators, we need to comprehend and address a complete range of cultural issues. To do this, we have to understand the values, customs and worldview of the dominant American culture as well as those of immigrant students and their families. We must be aware of the unique behaviors of each immigrant child, while appreciating and understanding the cultural context from which these behaviors originate. We should also try to understand the immigration experience and the process of acculturation — which is often painful and conflicting.

Immigrant Families Face Many Challenges

Significant life changes are always stressful, and can have serious physical and psychological effects, including anxiety, depression, sleep disturbances, and greater susceptibility to illness.

Think back on your own childhood and adolescence. Did you ever move to an unfamiliar city and enroll in a new school where you didn't know a single person? While still dealing with the loss of cherished friends and surroundings, you had to adjust to a new environment, establish new routines and attempt to make new friends.

Now imagine what it's like for an immigrant child. In addition to the normal stresses of moving, the newly arrived immigrant student must cope with multiple losses — country, customs, language, family, friends — and the trauma of migration itself. This experience can have a profound impact on the child's emotional, social and academic development.

Educators need to be familiar with common cultural stressors in order to help immigrant students and families through the healing and adjustment process.

Culture Shock — The Stress of Immigration

While the histories of immigrant students and their families differ in many ways, all share common characteristics. For each family, immigration was an exceedingly stressful experience, simultaneously offering hope for the future and threatening long-term instability.

- **Cultural and language differences.** The greater these differences, the more intense the shock and its emotional fallout.
- **Causes of migration.** Culture shock is greater when migration occurs suddenly as a result of political violence, war, or other catastrophes, with little opportunity for choice or planning.
- **Length of residency.** Generally speaking, the more recently an immigrant family's arrival in the U.S., the more intensely that family experiences the stress of migration.
- **Changes in socioeconomic status.** Very often immigration precipitates significant adjustments in income and social status, as families struggle to secure employment and affordable housing.

- **Lack of social networks.** Immigrant families often leave behind the very people they relied upon most for support and assistance. Until new relationships are formed, they may feel isolated and not know where to turn for help with basic necessities, like grocery shopping and medical care.

Traumatic Stress — Dealing with Memories of War, Torture, Separation and Deprivation

Some immigrant families have escaped from war-torn countries. Some have witnessed terrorist acts, experienced natural disasters, witnessed political violence or lived with constant threat of deprivation. These traumas add to the upheaval and psychological stressors of many newcomers to our school systems. If ignored or inadequately addressed, successful adaptation to our culture can be problematic, with serious consequences to immigrant students, families and the community.

After a traumatic event has been experienced and survived, it is not uncommon to experience "aftershocks" — strong emotional and physical reactions that can appear even weeks or months later. These reactions are normal; however, they don't *feel* normal and can be alarming to the person experiencing them, as well as to family and friends. Occasionally professional help is required to successfully manage symptoms of Post Traumatic Stress Disorder (PTSD), which may include:

- Re-experiencing events and/or associated feelings
- Anxiety

- Intense fear, helplessness, or loss of control
- Rage
- Depression
- Impulsive behavior
- Explosive episodes
- Flashbacks
- Restlessness
- Sleep disturbances
- Physical complaints
- Self-destructive behavior
- Suicidal thoughts or threats
- Substance abuse
- Sense of loss

Identity Crisis — Redefining Self in the New Environment

Though immigrant students and their families expect change, they often do not anticipate the extent to which life in this country will differ from their previous life. Ways in which people relate to each other are different. Schools and other institutions operate differently. Even simple daily tasks, such as shopping for food or asking for directions, can become challenges involving not only a language barrier, but the potential for cultural misunderstanding. Not surprisingly, many immigrants feel that their very identity is threatened in the new culture. Factors that can contribute to the severity of identity crisis include:

- **Generational disparity.** Intergenerational problems are often created when children become acculturated at a faster rate than their parents.
- **Expectations of the new culture.** Unrealistic expectations based on media images and popular misconceptions about life in the U.S. can lead to disillusionment when dispelled by reality.

- **Lack of self-esteem.** Even in the healthiest individuals, self-esteem is fluid, varying with events and social contexts, and can plummet in the aftermath of immigration.
- **Loss of control.** Immigrant students and their families often lack a sense of personal agency relative to decisions and events in their own lives, as they are steered through various bureaucratic mazes by dozens of relatively insensitive, if well-meaning, strangers.
- **Confusion.** When virtually everything is new, including, in many cases, the predominant language, it can be very difficult to stay clear and focused.

- **Anxiety.** Think of the anxiety you feel when something significant in your life abruptly changes and multiply that by a thousand.
- **Depression.** Multiple losses and feelings of powerlessness can lead to acute (temporary) or chronic (long term) depression.
- **Health problems.** Diet and climate changes, as well as stress can lower immune responses and make individuals more susceptible to illness.

Knowing the various types of challenges and stresses that immigrant students and families may experience will make it possible to more easily identify specific trouble spots and lend appropriate assistance. Immigrants can be expected to respond in a variety of ways depending on their expectations, their advance knowledge of this country, their eagerness to be here, and their emotional resiliency. Trauma is by no means inevitable, but some degree of difficulty ought to be expected.

Chapter 2

Understanding Cultural Differences

Becoming culturally skilled is an active and ongoing process. Given the complexity and diversity of the students and families in our school systems, we must continuously re-evaluate our approaches and learn new ways of observing, listening to and providing support for the newest members of the school community.

One of the first steps to becoming culturally skilled is to be conscious of our own culturally-based values, traits, practices and worldviews. Some are more obvious than others, so it doesn't hurt to do an accounting. For example, in America we emphasize individualism, egalitarianism and independence. The nuclear family is paramount; however, the roles of family members are flexible. Both parents participate in child rearing and domestic chores.

Power and opportunities are equal (or nearly equal) for both sexes, and most women are employed outside the home. We value competitiveness, democratic ideals, free market economics, mass media entertainment and material success. We are religious, but religion is constitutionally barred from government while freedom of individual religious expression is guaranteed.

Americans tend to be friendly, outgoing, outspoken, "in-your-face" people who enjoy having and voicing opinions, don't automatically defer to any age, group or class, and can be exceedingly compassionate and generous when their neighbors (both foreign and domestic) are in trouble.

Given this rough profile it is easy to see how an American teacher or counselor might view a modest, respectful Asian student as lacking in motivation or self-confidence. Or how a child from a less gregarious society might be seen as overly shy and withdrawn.

The cultural quiz at the end of this chapter provides thirty-seven examples of specific cultural dilemmas. You'll learn a great deal by looking at these situations, thinking them through, and then discovering the underlying issues.

As educators, we must be sensitive to and have knowledge of our own cultural and personal values, along with similarities and differences between ourselves and the immigrant families with whom we work. Several variables are worth keeping in mind when getting to know an immigrant student:

- rural/urban differences
- socioeconomic differences
- historical background
- religious beliefs and practices
- family educational levels
- language (monolingual, bilingual, multilingual)
- values/traditions
- levels of acculturation
- social class background
- gender roles and expectations
- attitudes toward assimilation

Identifying Cultural Values

In his landmark book, *Cultures Consequences* (2nd edition, Sage Publications, 2001), Dutch organizational anthropologist Geert Hofstede identifies four dimensions for defining values related to national culture: power distance, individualism/collectivism, masculinity/femininity, and uncertainty avoidance.

Hofstede's framework is widely used in international business and management, and to some degree in education, to draw comparisons between different cultural groups. Originally based on research conducted with middle class factory workers, Hofstede's theories have been validated repeatedly by other investigators and provide a useful analytical tool for understanding intercultural differences. Knowing about differences helps prevent conflict, and Hofstede's framework shows that it is not safe to assume that apparently similar countries in the same region, like Colombia and Venezuela for example, have similar cultures.

Hofstede defines culture as collective, but often intangible, and made up of two main elements: the internal values of the culture, which are largely invisible, and the external practices of a culture — rituals, heroes, symbols, etc. National cultures, according to Hofstede, can be differentiated by their values.

Since values are among the first things to be programmed into children, changing them later in life is difficult, which is one reason why immigrant students and their families often experience culture shock and difficulties acculturating.

Four Dimensions of National Culture

1. Power distance — how a society handles inequalities

Power distance is defined by Hofstede as the extent to which the less powerful members of institutions and organizations within a country *expect* and *accept* that power is distributed unequally.

In low power-distance nations, inequalities among people tend to be minimized and activities decentralized. For example, workers may expect to be consulted by their managers, students may have considerable choice about their classes and teachers, and parents may include children in family decisions. Conversely, in high power-distance nations, inequalities among people are considered desirable and power is centralized. This might mean that workers are isolated from their bosses, and teachers and parents have absolute authority in the classroom and home respectively.

2. Individualism vs. collectivism — behavior towards the group

Individualism is characterized by loose ties between individuals. People are expected to look out for themselves and their immediate family. Collectivism represents the opposite orientation, where people are integrated into strong, cohesive groups that provide a lifetime of mutual protection and support in exchange for loyalty.

In individualist societies (like the U.S.) loyalty and protection are not as important as individual freedom and opportunity. In collectivist societies, people need to belong to a group. Children from collectivist societies learn to think in terms of "we," whereas children in individualist societies learn to think in terms of "I."

3. Masculinity vs. femininity — behavior according to gender

These terms are misleading at first glance. Hofstede uses the term *masculine* to describe societies in which gender roles are separate and distinct. The term *feminine* pertains to societies in which gender roles overlap. So the U.S. is considered a feminine nation and Japan a masculine nation.

Western democracies have undergone a process of "feminization" in recent times, and researchers have pointed out that the emergence of developing countries is as much about feminization as it is about politics, business and economics.

4. Uncertainty avoidance — the need for structure

This is the extent to which members of a culture feel threatened by uncertain or unknown situations and therefore attempt to avoid them. Cultures with low uncertainty avoidance in general do not perceive something different to be dangerous. Conversely, cultures with high uncertainty avoidance impose lots of systems and rules to reduce the risk of uncertainty and maintain order.

A number of researchers have cast doubt on this dimension, suggesting that it may have been relevant only at the time Hofstede did his original research. Michael Bond, who took Hofstede's work to Hong Kong and Taiwan, identified a fifth dimension, long-term vs. short-term orientation. This dimension measures the extent to which a country takes a long or short term view of life.

Many educators, when evaluating the extent of cultural differences for a specific student or group of students, have found Hofstede's four dimensions a convenient, reliable tool. It should be used judiciously, but is certainly superior to hearsay and guesswork.

Ten Cultural Assumptions Counselors Make

The following list is borrowed from Paul Pederson (*A Handbook for Developing Multicultural Awareness*, 1994, American Counseling Association). The comments after each item represent the reactions of the author, and are not necessarily those of Pederson.

1. The concept of "normal" is universal.

It's not. What is considered normal varies over time and from culture to culture. Certain practices that are considered aberrant in the U.S. are perfectly acceptable in other societies.

2. The goal of counseling is to support individual growth and development.

Not necessarily. You may be working with a student from a collectivist country who finds the emphasis on individual achievement inappropriate, embarrassing, or even shameful.

3. Counselors know all they need to know to understand the client.

Even the most skillfully executed counseling techniques are rarely enough. This is especially true when working with immigrant students and families.

4. Clients understand linguistic abstractions, like fairness, truth, justice, good and evil.

In some cultures, such concepts only make sense within specific contexts, which tends to render them relative. For example, the truth about a situation may vary from one telling to the next, depending on who is listening.

5. Independence is desirable and dependence is not.

As Hofstede's framework illustrates, some cultures expect and accept inequality and dependence in certain relationships.

6. Client uses linear thinking and understands cause and effect.

People from fatalistic cultures adhere to the doctrine that all events are predetermined by fate (not cause and effect) and are therefore unalterable. In others cultures, beliefs are based on what many Westerners would consider vague, groundless speculation.

7. People with problems are assisted more by formal (professional) counseling than by informal support systems (family, friends).

Immigrants from collectivist cultures are often accustomed to having very strong support systems comprised of extended family and community. While much of this support may be lost during migration, that doesn't mean these clients are ready to substitute professional help. Many prefer to build new informal support networks.

8. Counselors need to help the individual adapt to social/educational institutions.

Not necessarily. Face it, there are some institutions to which none of us really wants to adapt. The important question is: Are the institutions serving the best interests of your client? If not, your role as a counselor is to advocate for the client. With immigrant families, acculturation (of which institutional adaptation is a part) takes time, so slow the pace and introduce change in small increments.

9. Here and now is more important than historical background.

It can be a huge mistake to ignore the past when dealing with immigrant students and their families. The past may hold keys to understanding the client's state of mind, values, behaviors, and worldview.

10. We already know our biases and culturally learned assumptions.

We may think we know them, but every human interaction (including every counseling relationship) holds the possibility of evoking an attitude or assumption heretofore unexamined. If we're open, we stand to learn as much about ourselves as we do our immigrant families.

Common Diversity Differences

Being aware of some of the common areas of cultural difference can go a long way in helping develop rapport and welcoming parents into the school community. Here are some areas where having an awareness can be very beneficial. It's still important to remember to never assume anything. There are still variations within cultures just as there are between cultures. Asking a cultural broker to inform you of the specific differences in the cultures you are working with can be most helpful.

Greetings: In the U.S. we generally greet people with a firm handshake, but this is not true for much of the rest of the world. The most common greeting in the world is the bow. It's important to know that in some cases a handshake can even be offensive. Men from the Middle East often shake hands with a slight bow and then exchange kisses on both cheeks. Traditional Muslim men might shake hands and then place the palm of their right hand over their heart as a sign of friendship. However they usually will not shake hands with a women and usually don't introduce women who are with them. It is not expected that you will shake the women's hand either.

Personal space: The comfortable space between people varies among different cultures. In the U.S. after a greeting and shaking hands we usually stand about two and a half feet apart. For those from formal countries this is often too close for comfort. In countries like Japan individuals bow and then take a step back. For Americans this might feel like a great distance, but if you move forward to close the gap the Japanese will usually take another step back to maintain the distance. Among many Hispanics and Middle Easterners, after a greeting and hug, this closeness is maintained. Most often, this is too close for most Americans who will feel uncomfortable and will take a step back. It seems in all this as if different cultures can "chase" each other around the room trying to find the comfortable distance within which to communicate.

Eye contact: Another difference is the amount of eye contact that is acceptable and comfortable among cultures. In the US we value a strong, direct, but non-threatening eye contact. Many Asians, Native Americans and some Hispanics avoid direct eye contact as a sign of respect.

Food: Understanding that food is culture specific can help when considering what foods to serve at parent nights or at other group meetings or events. Food is often an important item used to entice parents to come to the school for an event.

Understanding how some newly arrived immigrants (both adults and children) generally react to unfamiliar foods is also a good thing to keep in mind. In many cultures there is little or no dairy, red meat, or fried food. American food like pizza, burgers, and french fries may be totally unappealing. Adjust the food you serve to something that will be appealing to the cultures of your parents.

Culture Quiz

By Judie Haynes

The following scenarios are based on the actual experiences of Judie Haynes and her ESL colleagues. Test your knowledge of these common cultural dilemmas. For each problem consider what the underlying cultural issue is and what your solution might be. These situations also make excellent small-group discussion topics for inservice training, or to spark informal discussions with colleagues. After you have considered and/or discussed each situation, compare your answer with the author's. The answers are provided at the end of the quiz.

1. You are a 4th grade teacher with a new boy in your class from Syria. He speaks very little English. He is having a problem getting along with the other students. He has fights on the playground every day that he seems to provoke by constantly touching the other boys.

2. You have a new Korean girl in your 4th grade class. The other students in your class don't want to sit next to her because they say she smells funny. You have a bad allergy and can't tell. She appears

to be a clean, well-dressed child and you don't understand your students' objections.

3. You are a 3rd grade teacher who is having a parent conference with parents of an Asian student in your class. You explain to the parents that the child needs to spend more time working on his homework. The parents keep nodding and saying "yes" as you explain your reasons. You are disappointed when there doesn't seem to be any follow-up on the parents' part.

4. You are a 5th grade teacher who is using a lot of cooperative learning strategies in your classroom. In the middle of the year you get a new Syrian boy in your class. The student doesn't follow any of the rules you have explained through a bilingual classmate. He is very disruptive in your class.

5. You are a 6th grade teacher with your first student from China. She came with an excellent report card from her school in China. She is outstanding in math but can't seem to learn to read.

6. You are Ms. Smith, a 3rd grade teacher. You don't think your new student from Egypt is placed in the correct grade. You set up a meeting with the parents to discuss placing the child correctly. The father comes in to see you, but doesn't seem to take your concerns seriously.

7. You are a 1ˢᵗ grade teacher. A Korean student comes into your class in April. During a discussion of age and birthdays, this student says that she is eight years old. The other students in your class are turning seven. The office tells you that she has been correctly placed.

8. Guadalupe is a smiling 3ʳᵈ grader from Argentina. She seems well-mannered and eager to please. However, when you speak to her, she refuses to look at you.

9. You are a 4ᵗʰ grade teacher who wants to write a quick note home to an ESL student's family. You pick up the pen that you use to mark papers and write the note. When you hand the note to the student, she looks upset.

10. The Japanese mother of one of your 1ˢᵗ graders picks up her child every day at your door. You are upset because this mother seems unfriendly. She never smiles at you, and you wonder if you have done something to offend her.

11. Haitian brothers Jean-Baptiste and Jean-Pierre are often late for school. They are also each absent about once a week but on different days.

12. Your new Kurdish student seems to be sick all the time. He is lethargic and doesn't seem to even try to learn what you are teaching him.

13. A Russian student, who has learned English and is able to do much of the work in your 4th grade classroom, copies work from other students during tests. When you talk to him about this, he doesn't seem at all contrite. His parents act like you're making a big deal about nothing.

14. You have a Puerto Rican student in the 3rd grade who speaks English fluently. She participates orally in your classroom and socializes well with her peers. She even translates for other students. However, she is doing very poorly in her content area schoolwork.

15. Your 4th grade Malaysian student seems to be very good at Math. He gets "100" on his spelling tests. No one in your class knows the names of the state capitals better than he does. However, he seems to have a hard time comprehending a simple reading passage.

16. Some of your most advanced ESL students do not understand many of the geometric concepts that are taught in American classrooms from kindergarten.

17. Thi Lien is a new student from Viet Nam. She seems bright and alert, but gets no help from home. The papers you send home are still in her backpack the next day. Important correspondence is never acknowledged. She doesn't do homework and

forgets to bring back library books. Her home life appears to be very disorganized.

18. Pablo is a well-mannered boy from Colombia. He insists on calling you "Teacher" instead of your name, which you are sure he knows.

19. Hung is a bright ESL student in your 3rd grade class. He listens to you attentively and follows directions well. However, he is very rude when a classmate is speaking. He either talks to his neighbor or day dreams. He never joins in any class discussions.

20. You are a 3rd grade teacher. Your new Syrian student speaks Arabic. He seems to hold his pencil in a very clumsy way and has a great deal of difficulty even copying work in English.

21. Maria is a Mexican student whose attendance in your 6th grade class is very poor. It is affecting her academic performance. After an absence of several days, you ask her why she was out and she explains that her aunt was sick and her family went to help her. Although you explain the importance of good attendance in school, the same thing happens a few weeks later. You wonder if Maria's family considers education important.

22. Mei, a new student from China, is scheduled to begin your 4th grade class in the middle of the school year. On the day she registers, she is

introduced to your class and shown where she will sit. She is to begin school the next morning. You arrive in your classroom at 7:45 a.m. for a day that begins at 8:30. Mei is waiting at her desk in the dark. The custodian tells you that she arrived at 7:00 a.m.

23. Korean parents bring you a gift because you have helped their chid. You open it and thank them profusely for their generosity. The parents look upset.

24. You notice that a Muslim child in your classroom refuses to take a sheet of paper from a classmate. This isn't the first time this has occurred.

25. You have applied for a cultural trip for teachers to China. You know that you will be meeting other teachers along the way. You buy small gifts for them and wrap them in white tissue paper. At your first stop during the trip the recipients of your gifts seem upset.

26. Thu is a 6th grade girl from Thailand. She becomes hysterical when the other girls tease her by playfully mussing up her hair. Her parents have to come to school and take her home. While you understand her need to look tidy, you think she has overreacted.

27. During a parent conference, you tell the parents of your Colombian ESL student that their child is having difficulty learning English. You

suggest that they only speak English in their home. The parents look confused. When you relay this conversation to the ESL teacher in your school, she is very upset.

28. You are a 4th grade teacher. You have a friendly boy in your class from the Dominican Republic. He speaks very little English in the classroom and doesn't seem to be making much progress. When you give him directions, he seems to be confused. You are sure he is putting one over on you by pretending not to understand, because you have heard him speak with the other children on the playground.

29. You are a 4th grade math teacher. Ayumi is one of the brightest students in your class. She has been in the country for two years and it is obvious her background in math is superb. She can not seem to understand the units of fractions. You don't know what to think.

30. As a reward for good work in your class, you give students a packet of four pencils with decorative erasers as a gift at Christmas. Your Japanese students take two and leave two behind.

31. Jean Pierre is a 5th grade student from Haiti. Your class is studying long division. Jean-Pierre hands in his completed paper in a short time. You are upset because he has not completed the work. There is no work showing. You think the problem

is written backwards. Maybe the student has a perceptual problem.

32. An Egyptian student in your 3rd grade class is a good math student, but becomes disruptive when you teach a math lesson using math manipulatives.

33. You have a 3rd grade student from Bosnia. During recess time, the child hides under a bench and cannot be persuaded to come out.

34. You have a new 6th grade student from Asia. The student appears to have an attitude from the first day. Now he is out of his seat fooling around and you've just motioned him to come over to talk to you. He glares at you and seems even more angry.

35. Your 2nd grade class lines up for a field trip, and you count your students as you walk down the line, touching each of them on the head. You notice that several students pull back from you.

36. You take photographs of your students working in small groups for a Back to School Night. The grandmother of one of your Chinese students is very upset when she sees your photo of her granddaughter.

37. You signal "OK" by making a "O" with your thumb and forefinger to a student who has done a good job. Your 8th grade newcomer from Brazil looks very shocked.

Answers to Culture Quiz

1. American boys in grades 4-6 do not touch each other except during contact sports or when fighting. This is the way they are socialized. In Middle Eastern countries boys playing on a playground are constantly touching each other. When a Middle Eastern child does this on an American playground, he is likely to end up in many fights. The American boys see this as "sissy" behavior.

2. Different diets produce different body odors. Americans smell bad to some other cultures because they eat a lot of meat and milk. In the case of the Korean child, a diet heavy in garlic could be the reason for the odor.

3. Nodding and saying "yes" does not mean the parent agrees with you in Asian cultures. It means that they hear what you are saying. Most Asian parents would be too polite to disagree with the teacher.

4. This student could come from almost any culture. The organization of a cooperative learning classroom may look chaotic and undisciplined to new students. They can't tell what the rules are. This student probably came from a class where the teacher lectures and the student's role is more passive.

5. Unlike Japanese or Korean, the Chinese language has no sign/symbol correspondence. This basic reading concept is very difficult for students learning to read in English. Students need to go back to the beginning and learn to decode beginning phonics.

6. Often males from Middle Eastern countries have difficulty accepting a female teacher as a decision maker. Even if the family is not Muslim, very traditional roles for females are prevalent.

7. Everyone gains a year on the Lunar New Year. If a child is born in September, they will turn one in January or February, depending on the date of the Lunar New year. This student has counted her birthday as of January 25th. Many children lose a full year when they come to the U.S., and this needs to be explained to them.

8. In many cultures it is considered rude to look directly at an adult or a person considered of a higher status. This is so instilled in some students that they find it very difficult to learn to maintain eye contact.

9. Oops! You have used a red pen and written a note to the parents. This is very upsetting in many cultures where red is the color of death. Pay attention to this especially with your Korean students.

10. Japanese adults smile at friends and other people they know well. They do not use a smile as a way to say hello. Some Asian people seem to smile at everything. They feel it is correct to smile a lot like Americans, but they don't really know when a smile is appropriate in American culture.

11. They may be staying home on different days of the week to baby-sit for a younger sibling who does not yet attend school. They may be late because they have family obligations to help parents who are working. They may not have two sets of clean clothes that day.

12. Lethargy and illness are signs of culture shock. A student coming from a totally different culture and environment is going to be in shock. The greater the difference between the home culture and the American culture, the more severe these culture shock symptoms may be.

13. In many other cultures, copying from someone's paper does not receive the same reaction as it does in American culture. There is a lot of pressure on students to achieve any way they can. Many cultures in the previous "communistic block" countries see copying as a way of putting one over on the government. It is not considered "bad." American standards for academic honesty must be clearly explained.

14. This student has acquired BICS (Basic Interpersonal Communication Skills) but has not yet acquired CALPs (Cognitive Academic Language Proficiency) needed to learn in content areas. Many of our second language learners are exiting ESL programs at the BIC level. We need to work on CALPs before these students are exited. Good BIC skills also fool mainstream teachers, who think that a child speaking with friends on the playground is just being lazy when not doing his/her work.

15. The skills this student excels at are all "rote-memory" skills. This reflects the education of the student's country, where memorization and regurgitation are the way students learn. Asian students may become excellent at decoding words. Their parents think that they can read and they may even fool their teachers for a long time. They may not have good reading comprehension skills.

16. Math is not taught in a spiral manner in many other countries. American first grade math curricula introduces terms such as "cone" and "rectangular prism." Geometrical concepts are taught each year. Students from other countries may not learn much geometry before the 5th or 6th grade.

17. Many parents are working long hours to give their children a better life in America. They may get home very late. They may be

overwhelmed with their day-to-day routine. If your correspondence is in English, parents may not be able to read in English even if they speak it. Some parents may not be literate in their first language. It is important to keep this in mind.

18. In many cultures, it is rude to use the teacher's name. Respect is shown by addressing the teacher as "Teacher." When Pablo has enough English to understand, explain the American custom of using your name without the preface teacher.

19. In many cultures the teacher is the center of all learning. Other students are not seen as a source of information. These students need to be directly taught to listen to others, to express their own opinions, and join class discussions. One way to do this is to ask Hung what his classmate just said. If he doesn't know, have the classmate repeat it. Ask him if he agrees with someone's opinion.

20. This student is used to reading and writing from right to left, back to front. It will take longer to relearn this and to hold the pencil in a way that is appropriate for English writing.

21. Maria's family considers education important, but family obligations have a higher priority. Keep in constant communication with the parents.

22. Schools in many countries begin much earlier. Some schools in China begin at 7:00 or 7:30 in the morning. You need to have a translator or bilingual parent volunteer tell the student and her parents what time school starts.

23. Koreans consider it rude to open a gift in front of the giver. Gift giving is very serious business. You don't want to show any signs of lack of appreciation for the gift. In order to avoid this, gifts are not opened in the presence of the giver.

24. The student is probably handing the paper with her left hand. In many cultures the left hand is seen as "unclean." You don't hand people objects with it.

25. White is a sign of death or a funeral. Rewrap the gifts in red paper.

26. In Thai culture the head is where a person's soul resides. It is very important not to touch a child's head.

27. It is better for parents to speak a rich native language than fragmented English. Remember that any concept taught in native language will eventually translate to English. It is never appropriate to tell parents to speak only English in their home. If you moved to Japan, would you be able to speak only Japanese in your home?

28. The child has learned some BICS (Basic Interpersonal Communication Skills). He has not yet mastered academic language, which takes much longer.

29. Fractions are not very important in the rest of the world where the metric system is used. A fraction would be expressed in decimals.

30. Two is considered very lucky and four is very unlucky. Give gifts in twos.

31. This is the way division problems are written in Haiti and in many South American countries. Students in other parts of the world figure the problem out mentally. They do not write down the work.

32. Students from many other cultures will not be used to working with manipulatives. Students may become disruptive because they do not take this type of lesson seriously.

33. Children from war torn countries may be very sensitive to town whistles, ambulance and fire truck sirens, or even school bells. School staff members need to be aware of how frightening these sounds may be. Fire drill bells may cause a problem for any new students from countries where fire drills are not practiced.

34. The student is probably angry because he has had to move away from all that is familiar.

Culture shock plays a part in this behavior. How did you motion for the student to come over to you? Beckoning with one finger is rude in many cultures. It can be a gesture reserved for animals.

35. This is something primary teachers do all the time. To be on the safe side, refrain from touching Asian students on the head.

36. For conservative Chinese people, it is very bad luck to have a picture taken with an odd number of people. Three people in a picture is considered unlucky, especially for the person in the middle.

37. This typical American sign for "OK" is recognized in most of the world. However, it is very crude in a handful of countries, Brazil being one of them.

Some Final Guidelines

- Become well acquainted with the target population you are working with and learn about their culture, norms, values, traditions, attitudes and behaviors.
- Be aware of your own assumptions, values and biases.
- Understand the worldviews of culturally different students and their families.

- Develop and utilize culturally appropriate intervention strategies and techniques.
- Be aware of your own beliefs and attitudes regarding racial and ethnic minorities — your biases, stereotypes, and orientation toward multiculturalism.
- Know your own worldview.
- Use culturally appropriate intervention skills and strategies.

Excerpted from everythingESL.net, copyright Judie Hayes. For more great ideas visit the website www.everythingESL.net

Chapter 3

Communication

Excellent communication skills almost always cross cultural boundaries. What is effective with American children and their families is also effective with immigrant students and their families. The difference is, you may have to work a little harder. For example, instead of listening with 60 percent of your conscious attention (dividing the other 40 percent between various mental and environmental distractions), you may need to focus 95 percent. Instead of noting only obvious nonverbal behaviors, you may need to pay attention to numerous subtle clues. Instead of summarizing once at the end of the conversation, you may need to summarize at several intervals throughout the conversation.

However, aside from these differences of degree, the general rules of effective communication are universal.

As a listener...

- Give the other person your full attention.
- Demonstrate respect and sincere interest.
- Listen carefully, fully engaging both your mind and heart.
- Learn to recognize and interpret nonverbal signals (body language).
- Respond to show understanding (nod, paraphrase, etc.).
- Check for understanding.

As a speaker...

- Think before you speak.
- Choose your words carefully, using accurate terminology.
- Be concise and clear.
- Make sure your words and actions (body language) are congruent.
- Stop often and give the listener a chance to respond.
- Check for understanding.

If using an interpreter (or cultural broker — a role that will be discussed later), nothing much changes except the process takes longer. The bonus is that you have additional time (during translations) to watch for and interpret nonverbal signals.

Getting to know people of different cultures begins with trust and openness and a willingness to really listen. It means making a sincere effort to understand the true meaning of what the other person is saying. Much of the time we do this effortlessly with people who share our language and culture. With practice and effort, we can do it with people of different cultures as well.

Show that you value what the other person has to say. Keep an open mind, be aware of your biases, and exercise patience. Just about everything related to communication is likely to take longer — getting your point across, correctly interpreting the words and actions of the other person, and reaching agreements.

Demonstrate acceptance. You don't have to agree with the beliefs, perceptions, values or decisions of the other person, but you do need to believe and affirm that he or she is a worthwhile person.

Be trustworthy. Be open and honest and follow through on commitments. Always do what you say you are going to do.

Cultural Factors to Keep in Mind

Understanding your own culture is a major step toward understanding others. It's like anything else. Having a context and a basis for comparison makes identifying differences a lot easier. Remember that while values are the bedrock of culture, they often can only be understood by examining customs, communication styles and individual behaviors. The values themselves are hidden.

Communication styles and patterns, including body language, vary from one culture to another. For example, people from some cultures pull away in response to direct questioning or see "why" questions as accusations. Others feel an obligation to please the person with whom they are talking and think nothing of massaging the facts in order to do so. In some cultures, smiling and nodding have little to do with genuine pleasure or agreement. In others, having direct eye contact with someone in an authority position is considered rude.

In communicating with immigrant students and their families, it is important to do perception checks. Is your interpretation correct? Check with the other person. The rules for good listening and responding don't change, but if you are willing and able to make small adjustments in your *style* of communicating (to more closely mirror the style of the other person), communication will be improved.

The more you know about a student's culture, the better the chances of effective communication. This doesn't mean that you have to devote hours of study to becoming multiculturally literate. Showing an interest in the diverse experiences of students and their families is an important way to build relationships. Observing, asking questions and exploring differences in an open and honest way will go a long way to building insight and understanding. For example, questions and observations may tell you such things as:

- The amount of personal space an individual requires. (This tells you how much physical distance to allow between you and the other person.)
- How time is viewed. Does the American expectation of punctuality have meaning in the other culture? Is the fast pace of American life creating conflicts for the student or family? Do children and their parents understand and accept the concept of deadlines and due dates for projects and papers?
- The family's decision-making process. How does information seem to flow from the child to the home and back again to you? Is there an established protocol for gaining parent cooperation? Do family members other than parents (e.g., grandparents, aunts, siblings) need to be involved?

Gauge the amount of information you provide. This is particularly important when working with immigrant parents. Individuals experiencing culture shock are already overwhelmed. Piling on reams of information is probably going to be counterproductive. Prioritize what you need to convey to parents and then deal with it in small chunks. Have more contacts of shorter duration.

Using a Cultural Broker

A cultural broker is a person who knows the language, values, customs and traditions of two or more cultures and is able and willing to assist immigrant families and members of the host culture to understand one another, communicate productively and achieve whatever aims and objectives are appropriate at the time. Because the cultural broker is familiar with both cultures, he or she can point out differences and similarities and help bridge gaps caused by language, values and expectations.

ESL teachers often make good cultural brokers. So do some guidance counselors, religious leaders, representatives of community agencies that work with immigrant families, parent volunteers who share the immigrant's native language and culture, and students of the same culture who have been in the U.S. for some time.

The role of a cultural broker falls somewhere between that of an interpreter and a mediator. Interpreting language may be a major part of the responsibility, but it is just the beginning. Many other things may need translation, such as core beliefs, customs and accepted ways of doing things in each of the cultures. On the other hand, a cultural broker usually stops short of mediating conflicts, providing counseling or giving advice — unless, of course, the broker is a qualified counselor and has been asked by you to serve a mediator role.

Parent-Child Communications

Cultural brokers can be very helpful in bridging communication gaps that sometimes develop between immigrant students and their parents.

Children, particularly young children, often make lightening-quick progress in learning English and adopting American ways. In no time at all, a generation gap can develop between these

students and their parents. While the parents excel in the native language and honor old traditions, but lag in the new language and customs, the children become proficient in English, but have a poor command of their parents' language.

This communication gap may cause parents to feel they have lost control over, and respect from, their children. They may not be able to help with homework or communicate effectively with teachers and, as a result, may experience a loss of self-esteem.

The children, in the meantime, may feel rudderless — cut off from their parents, yet not fully at home in the new culture. They may feel embarrassed or resentful if repeatedly asked to translate during parent-educator meetings. Using a cultural broker in situations like these can take a lot of pressure off both students and their parents.

Parent-Educator Meetings

A major part of the communication between parents and teachers/counselors takes place in scheduled parent-educator conferences. This is as true for immigrant parents as it is for others, but in scheduling and conducting these meetings, some additional rules apply.

- If possible, phone immigrant parents at work, where they are more reachable. Then send a letter home the next day to confirm the meeting time and place.
- Schedule parent-teacher conferences on parents' days off.
- Send letters home weekly, describing what children have accomplished in school that week. Ask the children to read the letters to their parents and talk about what they are learning.
- If you work with several children who share the same language and culture, invite the parents of the those students to meet occasionally as a group. Have a cultural broker present, and talk about such things as recent classroom projects, special school activities, helping with homework, the importance of reading to/with the child, and community services.

Questions to Ask Immigrant Parents

Keep this list handy to remind yourself of specific areas of information that you need to cover when talking with the families of immigrant students.

Family history

- Who are the members of your family?
- How many are here in the U.S. and how many are still in your homeland?
- Why did you immigrate?
- How was life in your country of origin different from the life you have now?
- What are some of the things you miss most about your homeland?

Language

- How many people speak English in your home? What other languages are spoken?
- What do family members read?
- Do parents read to the children at home? In what languages?
- What are the favorite stories of your children?

Home life

- Describe a typical weekday in the life of your child. What are weekends like?
- What kinds of things does the family do together?
- Does the child spend time alone?
- In what activities do children participate (art, drama, music, sports, science, etc.)?

School expectations

- What are your educational expectations for your children?
- How do you think your children learn best?
- What was the educational system like in your homeland?
- What was the role of teachers? ...parents? ... principals?

- Was counseling available?
- How much time does your child have to study?
- How much help does your child get with homework?
- What can the teacher do to help your child learn in the classroom?
- What are your major concerns?
- How do parents get involved in the education of their children in your homeland?

Community and its resources

- How do you find out about community events?
- What community events do you participate in?
- What areas of information do you need (e.g., health, housing, jobs, social services, education, religion)? How do you currently get this information?

Areas of expertise

- What abilities and talents do you have?
- What was your work in your country of origin?
- What are your hobbies?
- What kind of work are you doing now?
- What musical instruments do you play?

Building Rapport

Establishing rapport with immigrant parents is an integral part of the relationship-building process. Taking time to establish this rapport right from the start will make the long-term relationship between parents and school personnel more successful. All people want to feel important, valued, and as if they belong. When there is good rapport, it means that the people involved in the relationship relate well to one another and can interact without difficulty. Here are some tips for building quality rapport with immigrant parents

1. Be a good listener: After you ask a question, allow plenty of time for the parent to respond. The parent may need time to process the question or simply do some mental translation from one language to another. Be patient, open, and encouraging in your demeanor and body language. Show interest and non-judgment in the answers.
2. Be interested: People generally like and trust others who are interested in them. We all feel connected and valued when someone pays attention to us. Ask questions (being sensitive

to cultural norms). Get to know the parents, where they have come from, what their interests, experiences, and abilities are, what they do for a living in the U.S. Explore the dreams they have for their children and family.

3. Be a mirror: We generally feel comfortable with, and relate well to others who are like us. One way we show our similarities, regardless of cultural background, is to mirror the demeanor and other communication cues of the person with whom we are speaking. Observe the style of the parent. Is he, or she, slow and deliberate, or exuberant and quick? Watch the breathing patterns, body language, speed at which words are spoken, open or closed posture etc. As much as possible, get into sync with the patent.

4. Stay focused: If you are distracted when meeting with parents, it will show, and that says you're more interested in what is distracting you than the parents. Developing rapport requires that you pay attention. Nothing can distance a parent more than the feeling of not being important enough to be paid attention to. Set all meetings up so that you are away from distractions – and remember to turn off your cell phone.

Chapter 4

Ideas for Reaching Out to Immigrant Parents.

Parent involvement is an ideal we strongly promote in the U.S., but sometimes it takes a lot of encouragement to convince immigrant parents that their participation is desired and valuable. Education differs markedly from one country to another and, in some, parents are given no voice in the subjects their children study or anything else about the system. The notion of a home-school partnership may be completely new and strange.

Other serious blocks to parental involvement include work hours, lack of parental self-confidence, poor English-language skills and unfamiliarity with the school system and its goals. It's up to the school to set a consistent welcoming tone that will eventually convince immigrant parents and families to become involved in their children's education. The strategies should include the following:

- Promote and convey the belief that all parents have something valuable to contribute to the education of their children.
- Encourage parents to have a role in the school and in the classroom.
- Recognize the efforts of caring and involved parents.
- Establish parent support groups.
- Offer parent leadership-training classes.
- Involve parent and teacher associations in welcoming and supporting newly arrived immigrant students.

Collaborative efforts with parents result in students with greater motivation, improved behavior and higher academic achievement. You have an opportunity to incorporate parents in full partnership in the education of their children and offer adults new to this country a vision of opportunities available to them. Parents, in turn, can then be counted on to communicate these same opportunities to their children.

From the First Moment...

Develop procedures for receiving and orienting newcomers to the school. Having these in place well ahead of time makes it easy to shift into a welcoming mode when a new immigrant student arrives.

- Immigrant parents feel welcomed when they know someone within the school. Help create relationships between staff and parents, and among parents.
- Actively reaching out to immigrant parents through home visits and phone calls can be highly effective means of engagement.
- Create welcome signs and banners in the languages of the community and display them in strategic locations around the school.
- Train office and support staff to receive new students in a welcoming manner, and to set in motion appropriate activities to help the family become oriented and receive necessary information.
- Form a welcoming team made up of the principal and several staff members. Get enough people on the team to ensure that at

least two are available at any given time. Post a rotation schedule, so that office staff can quickly contact members of the team and call them to the office when a new student arrives.

- Use an interpreter (or cultural broker) who is competent in the language and culture of the newcomer, and has a thorough understanding of the school system. Studies have found that bilingual school staff who purposefully engage immigrant parents have been successful at getting parents to attend activities and events.

- Ensure that the interpreters are supported and have the necessary resources to effectively meet their responsibilities.

- Allow ample time for the first interview. Communicating through an interpreter can easily double the amount of time required to take the child and family through the registration and orientation process. Scheduling extra time in advance helps ensure a relaxed and enjoyable meeting.

- Provide basic information about the length and structure of the school day, the school calendar, what the student needs to bring to school (books, materials, lunch, etc.), and available transportation services.

- Do not overload the family with information during this first meeting. Establish a relationship with the parents so that orientation can continue during the weeks and months ahead.
- Be sure that all the information you present verbally is also given to the family in printed form. A good way to accomplish this is to publish a "welcome booklet" in representative

languages. Keep it simple, but include information about the school program, the structure of the school day and year, absence and re-admittance procedures, special activities and events, holidays, and the role parents are encouraged to take. Include a page for personalized information, where you can write in the names of the principal, the child's classroom teacher and second-language teacher, and important phone numbers. Also keep parents informed of other resources and oppotunities their families can benefit from such as ESL classes and tutoring.

- Another important point to remember is that some immigrant parents may not be literate in their native languages either. It's important to provide guidance and information in ways that each parent can understand.
- Provide the student with a "starter kit" of materials, including pencils, colored markers, ruler, eraser, notebook, picture dictionary, etc.
- Escort the family on a brief school tour. Include a visit to the student's classroom and the second language room.
- Introduce the family to the grade-level teacher, the second language teacher, and a student "ambassador" from the same class.

After the Initial Meeting

Eventually, immigrant families must be familiar with all aspects of the American system of education. Cover additional information gradually in subsequent meetings or in parent support groups. Important topics might include:

- Academic requirements, subject requirements, grading system, marking system, special programs, electives and extracurricular activities
- Student rights and responsibilities
- Parent rights and responsibilities
- Services for immigrant students, e.g., orientation and ambassador programs, bilingual program, English as a second language program
- Organizational chart of school and/or district, including names, titles and phone numbers
- After school programs
- Scholarship programs
- Transcript evaluations (equivalence of foreign and American coursework)
- Health information, including child insurance and special health services for immigrant families
- Grievance procedures

Additional Ideas for the School

- Create a reproducible community map showing social services, educational services, health services, housing services, immigrant services, and more.
- Create a "resource center" for immigrant parents, possibly staffed by other immigrant parents. Offer orientation programs covering essential services in the community, information about the school and its programs, after school activities, child care and health services. Set appropriate hours so that working parents can visit the center. Consider offering parent leadership classes and providing internet access.
- Generate a bulletin board listing jobs, community resources, school programs and activities, essential phone numbers and other information, including a community map.
- Set aside funds to assist immigrant families who have difficulty providing school supplies and clothing.
- Organize a clothing exchange. To eliminate the risk of donor's re-encountering their own items, used clothing collected in one area of the district can be sent to another area for sale

in a reuse clothing "store," where items are attractively displayed.

- Immigrant parents are often interested in sharing their experiences. Solicit the names of parents who are willing to share their expertise, talents or interests on career days or at other special events. Maintain a list of such parents, including nationality, language, talents/skills and availability. Have parents from particular occupational areas do demonstrations and talk about their professions.

- In a New Haven school, second graders have created a "café" where they periodically prepare a meal and honor a special "celebrity guest," often the parent or grandparent of one of the students. When using this idea to honor immigrant family members, prepare foods representative of the guest's native culture and invite a cultural broker to translate.

- When school starts each year, write a note to families introducing yourself and asking them to share their special talents, interests and hobbies with your class. Include a volunteer form and then be sure to follow up on all responses. Send correspondence in the first language of the parents.

- Tell families how the school system works and what it can do for them. Many parents, especially immigrant parents, are not aware of all the services available in schools. In the language of the parents, explain the role of counselors, psychologists, health-care professionals, and other specialists. Explain how the system is structured and how people in different roles work together to ensure a quality education for their children.

- Listen to parents, even when they are upset or angry. Involve cultural brokers to help bridge communication gaps. Be open to fresh perspectives and insights that you and your colleagues haven't considered.

- Ask the PTA to host regular before-school and after-work coffees for parents. No particular agenda is necessary for these informal drop-in events — only generous participation of staff, so that parents who do stop by can mingle, get better acquainted, and build a feeling of partnership with the school. In addition to coffee and donuts, include a beverage and snack from a different culture at each gathering.

- Organize and promote parent peer-group meetings. In one school, parents of 5th and 6th graders get together occasionally to talk about issues that are important in the development and schooling of their 10 and 11 year olds

- Occasionally invite a professional to attend and discuss a particular subject, like child rearing. Include a cultural broker. Peer group topics might include:
  — Available community language programs
  — Accessing medical services
  — Housing facilities and services
  — Shopping facilities
  — Using available recreational activities
  — Interacting with the school
  — Disciplining children
  — Effective communication and family relationships
  — Conflict management
  — Relating to the past, the native country, and distant relatives and friends
- Invite immigrant parents to participate in the school's parent-advisory council meetings. Explain that the council represents the school's parents and makes recommendations to the principal and school board. Promote the council as an outlet for parent concerns, making sure to include cultural brokers so that cross-cultural understanding is assured and the input of immigrant parents is given full consideration.

Ideas for the Classroom

Immigrant students adjust to classroom routines and expectations more easily if the class and the teacher already have procedures in place for welcoming the newcomer and integrating him or her into the class. The following suggestions are intended to make the classroom an inviting, inclusive, culturally sensitive learning environment for all children of all cultures.

- When you introduce immigrant students, tell the class what country they are from, what language they speak, and explain that they are learning to speak English. Avoid referring to the child as language deficient or handicapped in any way.
- Translate and explain important announcements to newcomers. For example, make sure that immigrant students know about holidays and professional activity days when school is closed, so that working parents can make arrangements to have their children supervised.
- Work hard to prevent prejudice and discrimination. Teach students about the dangers of stereotyping, name-calling and exclusion. Model and promote tolerance and inclusion.

- Incorporate multicultural images and expressions into your teaching. Use words and phrases from other languages, including metaphors and proverbs.
- When talking with immigrant parents about their child, begin and end with something positive. The same is true when dealing directly with the child. Instead of commenting primarily on areas that need work, point out strengths and achievements, no matter how small. A good ratio is three positive to one negative. Catch the student doing something right.

- Aim for frequent, consistent communication. Instead of sending home an occasional newsletter or note, include a place for comments (yours and the parents') on each day's assignment, and in the appropriate language. You don't always have to write something, but immigrant parents will appreciate knowing that they always have an opportunity to respond.

- Hold a class celebration on the birthdays of cultural icons and heroes. Celebrate authors, artists, musicians, scientists, political figures, social activists and others. Have the students research each honoree and share information about the person during the celebration.

- Help immigrant parents create a home environment which supports learning and literacy for the children. Cover such things as providing a quiet space for children to study and to be consistent in devoting time to study. Encourage parents to read to their children, if possible in English, or their native languages

The World Since 9/11

The horrific events of 9/11/01 have changed Americans forever. In the years since this disaster, many of us have felt bewildered and dismayed at the level of rage against Americans that precipitated these events, and have wondered what we can do to help prevent future terrorist acts.

Here is one simple thing that we can do to help: Make school safe for all children.

Although immigrant families may not support the views of the U.S. prevalent in their native countries, they are sometimes labeled, stereotyped and ostracized nonetheless, just because they are (or appear to be) Arab, or because they wear a turban or a scarf. Immigrant children may experience discrimination in school, and may feel fearful or ashamed, concluding with childish innocence that they come from "bad" people or "evil" places.

Fear has become a subtle, but steady, undercurrent in our cities and public places. We share a new alertness. Ironically, certain immigrants are discovering themselves to be objects of the wariness felt by all of us. They not only fear terrorist attacks, they fear reprisals against those associated with terrorist attacks. It's an odd conundrum, especially for individuals who are already dealing with the riddles and contradictions of a new culture.

We need to address these concerns with immigrant parents in peer-group meetings and at other appropriate gatherings. We can give families an opportunity to talk about their fears and concerns by asking questions that spark discussion without generating defensiveness. Here are some possibilities:

- Do you have concerns about how people think of each other since the events of 9/11?
- What can the school do to ease your concerns?
- How are you being treated in the community?
- How are your children being treated in school?
- What do you do to feel safe when there are dangers around?
- How do you find peaceful places in yourself, your family, the neighborhood, and the school?
- What are some things you can tell your children about how to feel safe and secure?

As we generate discussion and dialogue, we need to be extra sensitive to the messages immigrants give us and, more importantly, to the messages we ourselves convey through our individual and collective behavior.

Those of us who work with immigrant students and their families are uniquely positioned to help develop understanding, tolerance and peaceful dialogue in our school communities and neighborhoods. Let's not miss this opportunity.

Encourage Parents to Read to Their Children

Encourage parents to read to their children (or, if the parents are unable to read English, have the children read aloud to them). This is one of the most important things that parents can be encouraged to do. The 1985 report "Becoming a Nation of Readers" found that "the single most important activity for building the knowledge required for eventual success is reading aloud to children."

On the following page is a list of ten benefits produced by regular parent-child reading sessions. This page is designed as a handout to be reproduced and distributed to English speaking and/or reading parents.

For those parents who do not speak and/or read English ask an interpreter or cultural broker to translate the "ten reasons" into the family's native language, using the English version as a guide. Provide this list to the non-English speaking and/or reading families.

Ten reasons you should read to your child every day, or have your child read to you . . .

1. Reading helps build family unity.

2. Reading helps children solve problems and make good decisions.

3. Reading can help children understand and handle difficult situations.

4. Reading teaches children good communication skills and how to express themselves well.

5. Reading to children helps them learn to be good readers.

6. Reading raises academic performance.

7. Reading teaches responsibility, develops integrity and good character.

8. Reading helps children learn new words.

9. Reading builds self-confidence and self-respect.

10. Reading shares wisdom and information with children.

About The Author

Cristina Casanova is a licensed counselor who has worked with adults, children and adolescents for 35 years. During the past ten years, Ms. Casanova has been training school counselors in the New York City Public Schools in mediation, crisis response, cross cultural counseling, conflict resolution, and group, trauma, and grief counseling.

Ms. Casanova, holds an M.A.; M.Ed. in Counseling Psychology from Columbia University, and is a licensed mediator for New York State. Cristina produced the award-winning, first bilingual video and manual on mediation for adolescents in the United States. She has studied multicultural issues with Jean Houston, Paul Pederson and Samuel Johnson, and has facilitated thousands of workshops on cross-cultural counseling and immigrant issues.

Cristina is a senior faculty member for Group Works and the Applied Psychology Department of New York University. She is a consultant in trauma resolution issues for Group Works, Inc., as well as a trainer for the Child Trauma Institute. Ms. Casanova has facilitated hundreds of workshops on Trauma and Systemic Family Constellation in the United States, Ukraine, Belgium, Spain and Mexico. She also maintains a private practice with an emphasis on integrative therapy and trauma healing.

If your heart is in Social-Emotional
Learning, visit us online.

Come see us at
www.InnerchoicePublishing.com

Our web site gives you a look at all our other Social-Emotional
Learning-based books, free activities, articles, research, and
learning and teaching strategies. Every week you'll get a new
Sharing Circle topic and lesson.

INNERCHOICE Publishing

15079 Oak Chase Court
Wellington, FL 33414

www.ingramcontent.com/pod-product-compliance
Lightning Source LLC
Chambersburg PA
CBHW060440090426
42733CB00011B/2341